Play Piano Today!

A Complete Guide to the Basics

by Warren Wiegratz and Michael Mueller

Recorded at Beat House, Milwaukee, Wisconsin

ISBN 0-634-02852-9

HAL•LEONARD®
CORPORATION

7777 W. BLUEMOUND RD. P.O. BOX 13819 MILWAUKEE, WI 53213

Visit Hal Leonard Online at
www.halleonard.com

Introduction

Welcome to *Play Piano Today!*—the series designed to prepare you for any style of piano playing, from rock to blues to jazz to classical. Whatever your taste in music, *Play Piano Today!* will give you the start you need.

About the CD

It's easy and fun to play piano, and the accompanying CD will make your learning more enjoyable, as we take you step by step through each lesson and play each song along with a full band. Much like with a traditional lesson, the best way to learn this material is to read and practice a while first on your own, then listen to the CD. *Play Piano Today!* is designed to allow you to learn at your own pace. If there is ever something that you don't quite understand the first time through, go back on the CD and listen again. Every musical track has been given a track number, so if you want to practice a song again, you can find it right away. Additionally, the piano tracks on the CD are panned to the right in the mix, and the band tracks are panned to the left. This allows you not only to isolate the piano for learning parts without hearing the band but to isolate the band so that you can play along once you've learned the piano part.

Contents

Lesson 1 | The Blues

The blues is a truly American music form—and one of the most fun styles to play. Blues songs follow a standard formula of chord changes called the I–IV–V progression; that is, the first, fourth, and fifth chords in a given key. In the key of C, the chords would be C, F, and G7.

The melodies in blues songs come from the notes in the **blues scale**. Like the major scale, the blues scale contains seven notes, but it requires a new fingering pattern.

Track 2

C Blues Scale

Track 3

G Blues Scale

There are twelve measures in one chorus of the blues, hence the term **12-bar blues**. The formula is as follows: Four measures of the I chord; two measures of the IV chord; two measures of the I chord; one measure of the V chord; one measure of the IV chord; one measure of the I chord; and one measure of the V chord. You can see this pattern in each of the next two songs.

Track 4

Blues in C

The G3 Blues

Lesson 2 Accents

When listening to almost any form of music, you'll notice that some notes are played louder than others. These are accented notes. An *accent* is defined as emphasizing or stressing a particular note. On the piano, this is done by playing the note slightly louder than nonaccented notes. An accent is indicated by the symbol > placed at the notehead, like this:

So, whenever you see the accent symbol in the next song, "Movin' to Motown," play the indicated note slightly louder.

Track 6

Movin' to Motown

Did your accents match those on the CD? Good, move on to the next song, "Accentuate."

Track 7

Accentuate

Sixteenth Notes

In *Play Piano Today! Level 1*, you learned how to subdivide notes from a whole note, which gets four beats, all the way down to an eighth note, which receives half of a beat. Now we're going to move to a note of even shorter duration: the sixteenth note.

The sixteenth note is one half the duration of an eighth note, and there are four sixteenth notes in one beat. Sixteenth notes are notated like quarter notes, but they have two flags. Or, you can think of it like an eighth note with an extra flag. For two or more consecutive sixteenth notes in one beat, you can beam them together like eighth notes but with two beams.

To properly count the rhythm of sixteenth notes, count "one-ee-and-uh, two-ee-and-uh," etc.

1 e & a 2 e & a 3 e & a 4 e & a

Sixteenth notes can also be combined with eighth notes in the space of one beat. Try the next example to get a feel for sixteenth-note rhythms, and then play the next song, "Fall on Me."

Track 8

Sixteenth-Note Rhythms

Track 9

Fall on Me

Low E

The low E note is played with your left-hand pinky finger in E position and sits on the first ledger line beneath the staff in bass clef.

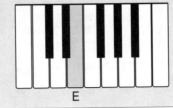

Low E Song

House of the Rising Sun

Here's a funk song that incorporates the low E note, sixteenth-note rhythms, and accents.

A Minor Funky

Sixteenth and Dotted Eighth Rests

The sixteenth-note rest has the same duration as a sixteenth note. It can appear on any of the four sixteenth-note subdivisions of a single beat and is counted in the same manner as a sixteenth note.

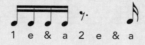

A sixteenth rest can also be added to an eighth rest by placing a dot next to the eighth rest. This is called a dotted eighth rest. The dotted eighth rest is the equivalent of three sixteenth rests and is most easily counted using sixteenth-note subdivisions.

Sixteenth-Note Rests

► Don't lose track of the downbeat! Listen for the metronome and let it be your guide.

Track 14

Arrested

Track 15

Give Me a Rest

Notes A, B, and C

In the treble clef, the high A note occupies the first ledger line above the staff; B is in the space above the first ledger line; and C sits on the second ledger line above the staff.

G Position

The A, B, and C notes are played with the index, middle, and ring fingers, respectively, with your right hand in G position an octave plus a 5th above middle C.

Here's a short melody for you to practice reading these new notes and playing in this new position.

Track 16

ABC Song

Track 17

Snow Fall

► Remember to perform a cross-under with your left thumb in measure 1.

Track 18

The Bells of Capetown

Eighth-Note Triplets

You've previously learned that if you divide a quarter note in half, you get two eighth notes, and if you divide a quarter note by four, you get four sixteenth notes. If you divide a quarter note into three equal subdivisions, the result is an *eighth-note triplet.*

Eighth-note triplets are notated as three eighth notes beamed together with a number 3 placed above or below the beam.

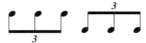

To count a triplet, you can either count: "One-and-a, Two-and-a, etc." or simply say the word "tri-pl-et" for each beat.

count: One- and - uh Two - and - uh Tri - pl - et Tri - pl - et

Track 19

Eighth-Note Triplets

Track 20

Jesu, Joy of Man's Desiring

► Use the "one-and-uh," two-and-uh" counting method to help you keep your place in the music when you encounter a lot of triplets in a song.

Three for Me

Quarter-Note Triplets

If you divide a half note into three equal subdivisions, the result is a **quarter-note triplet**. The quarter-note triplet is notated as three quarter notes with a bracket placed at the stem and the number 3 in the middle of the bracket.

Counting quarter-note triplets is a little trickier than eighth-note triplets. You can think of a quarter-note triplet as playing every other note of an eighth-note triplet.

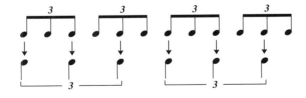

Quarter-Note Triplets

Be sure you're confident playing the quarter-note rhythm in the previous example before moving on to the next song.

Track 23

Triplet Song

Triplet Rests

Triplets can also contain rests. The most common rest placement within a triplet is the middle beat. This creates the **shuffle** feel that is commonly heard in blues and rock music.

Rests may appear on other portions of the triplet as well.

Track 24

Triplet Rests

Cranberry

Lesson 6 — New Chords

Em, Am, and B7

The Em, Am, and B7 chords are the three main chords in the key of E minor. The Em chord contains the notes E, G, and B. It is played with fingers 5, 3, and 1 on your left hand, and with fingers 1, 3, and 5 on your right hand.

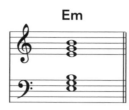 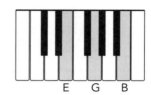

The Am chord contains the notes A, C, and E. It is played with fingers 5, 2, and 1 on your left hand, and with fingers 1, 4, and 5 on your right hand.

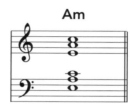 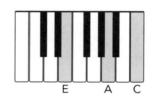

The B7 chord contains the notes B, D#, and A. It is played with fingers 5, 2, and 1 on your left hand, and with fingers 1, 4, and 5 on your right hand.

 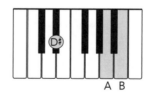

 Track 26

Right Hand

 Track 27

Left Hand

18

Lotus Blossom Spring

► Be mindful of the various hand-position shifts and fingerings in the right hand. Take special note of the thumb on the D♯ note three measures from the end.

D.C. al Fine

In Level 1, you learned notation shortcuts such as the repeat sign and first and second endings. Another useful direction is *da capo al fine*, or **D.C. al Fine**, for short. When you see this placed above the staff, you should return to the beginning of the piece and play until you reach the Fine sign, which ends the piece.

Funky Danube

Lesson 7 6/8 & 12/8 Time Signatures

Up until this point, you've played only meters in which the quarter note got the beat (4/4 and 3/4). In 6/8 or 12/8 time, however, the eighth note gets the pulse. In 6/8 time, it's easiest to count "one-two-three-four-five-six" for each measure.

count: one two three four five six

In 12/8, even though the eighth note equals one beat, the pulse is typically felt more like four groups of three, so count 12/8 as such: "One-two-three, Two-two-three, Three-two-three, Four-two-three."

count: **1** - 2 - 3 **2** - 2 - 3 **3** - 2 - 3 **4** - 2 - 3

Track 30

6/8

count: 1 - 2 - 3 - 4 - 5 - 6   1 - 2 - 3 - 4 - 5 - 6   1 - 2 - 3 - 4 - 5 - 6   1 - 2 - 3 - 4 - 5 - 6

Track 31

12/8

count: **1** - 2 - 3 **2** - 2 - 3 **3** - 2 - 3 **4** - 2 - 3   **1** - 2 - 3 **2** - 2 - 3 **3** - 2 - 3 **4** - 2 - 3

Track 32

Greensleeves

► Pay close attention to the fingerings.

Earlier, we discussed the shuffle rhythm as an eighth-note triplet with a rest on the middle eighth note. The shuffle can also be felt in 12/8 by dividing the measure into four pulses comprised of a quarter note and an eighth note.

Shuffle to Toledo

Fermata and Ritardando

The *fermata* symbol (⌢) indicates a hold or a pause. It is typically found at the end of a song and allows for a "big finish" by holding a note for an extended period of time. Since it's often the last note or chord of the song, holding it for an extended period has no bearing on the rhythm or time.

A *ritardando*, or *ritard* for short, indicates a gradual slowing of the tempo, usually at the end of a piece. Used in conjunction with a fermata, you can bring a song to a dramatic close. Listen to the next song, "Ballroom Ballad," for an example.

Track 34

Ballroom Ballad

Lesson 8 | Key of D

In *Level 1*, you learned the C, G, and F major scales. It's now time to add D major to your arsenal. The D major scale contains two sharps, F♯ and C♯, and is spelled D–E–F♯–G–A–B–C♯. To play the D major scale with your right hand, begin with finger 1 on the D note and play the first three notes (D, E, F♯). Then, perform a cross under to place your thumb on the G note and play the remaining five notes. To descend the scale, play the first five notes in position, then cross finger 3 over your thumb to play F♯ and finish the scale with fingers 2 and 1.

Track 35

With your left-hand pinky finger on the low D note, play the first five notes of the scale in position. Then, cross over with finger 3 to play the B note and finish the scale with fingers 2 and 1. When you descend, play D–C♯–B, then cross finger 1 under to play the A note and finish the scale with your remaining fingers in position.

Track 36

Track 37

Funk Rock a My Soul

24

D, G, A7

Here are the primary chord voicings in the key of D major: D, G, and A7. The D major chord contains the notes D, F♯, and A. It is played with fingers 1, 3, and 5 on your left hand, and with fingers 1, 3, and 5 on your right hand.

 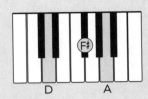

The G major chord contains the notes G, B, and D. It is played with fingers 5, 4, and 1 on your left hand, and with fingers 1, 4, and 5 on your right hand.

 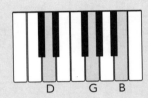

The A7 chord contains the notes A, C♯, and G. It is played with fingers 5, 4, and 1 on your left hand, and with fingers 1, 4, and 5 on your right hand.

 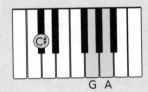

Track 38

Left Hand

Track 39

Right Hand

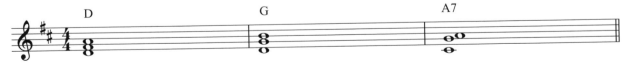

The Lonesome Prairie

Fine

D.C. al Fine

New Note: D

The high D note occupies the third space above the staff (space above second ledger line) in treble clef and is two octaves plus a major second above middle C. It is played with your pinky finger when you're in G position.

In the bass clef, the low D note occupies the space below the first ledger line below the staff. It is played with the pinky finger on your left hand.

Luggin' It

D.S. al Coda

Another very common notation shortcut is *dal segno al coda*, or **D.S. al Coda**. When you see this above the staff, return to the sign (𝄋) and play to the "To Coda" instruction. At that point, you skip ahead to the coda, indicated by (⊕), and finish the piece.

Track 42

Brahms in Jamaica

► Play the first section through the first ending, then repeat and take the second ending until you reach the D.S. al Coda indication. Go back to the sign, play the first six measures, and at the To Coda indication, skip to the coda and finish the song.

28

Bm and F#7

The Bm chord contains the notes B, D, and F#. It is played with fingers 1, 3, and 5 on your left hand, and with fingers 1, 3, and 5 on your right hand.

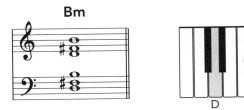

The F#7 chord contains the notes F#, A#, and E. It is played with fingers 4, 3, and 1 on your left hand, and with fingers 1, 2, and 4 on your right hand.

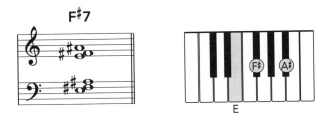

More Accents and Articulations

The **tenuto** articulation is marked by a hypen-like symbol at the notehead: ♩. The tenuto indicates that you must hold the note for its full value. It is often found on the first of two eighth notes in a phrase.

The **sforzando** is an accent marked by a symbol that looks like an inverted V: ∧. The sforzando, or *sfz*, indicates that the note should be played with a particularly strong accent and held slightly shorter than its full value. You may find these at the end of a song or the end of a section.

Track 43

La Perla

Lesson 9 The Chromatic Scale

The chromatic scale is made up of half steps and contains all twelve notes in an octave. Because it contains every note, there is only one chromatic scale. For our purposes, we'll start on the note C. Regardless of whether you're playing with your left or right hand, play all the black keys with finger 3 and all the white keys with finger 1, except when there are two consecutive white keys (E–F and B–C). In these two cases, use finger 2 to play the second white key when ascending with the right hand and the first white key when descending with the right hand. With the left hand, simply do the opposite. Play the first of two consecutive white keys with finger 2 when ascending and the second white key when descending.

Right Hand Chromatic Scale

Track 44

Left Hand Chromatic Scale

Track 45

Chromatic Soul

Track 46

Track 47

The Jester's Dance

► In the second-to-last measure, the right hand part ascends the scale, while the left hand part descends the scale. This is called *contrary motion.*

Special Techniques

Glissando

The *glissando*, or *gliss*, is a piano technique in which you slide your finger from one note to another, dragging it across the other keys in between. For an ascending glissando, drag your index finger or index and middle fingers together across the keys to the target note. Your hand should be turned so that your fingernails are in contact with the keys. For a descending glissando, drag your thumb (thumbnail side in contact with the keys) down to the target note.

ascending glissando

descending glissando

Glissandos are typically used to move between notes that are one or two octaves apart but can be used with other intervals as well.

Track 48

C to G

Track 49

C to C

Gliss Bliss

New Note: E

The high E note is two octaves plus a major 3rd above middle C. It occupies the third ledger line above the staff in treble clef.

The high E note in the left hand is a major third above middle C and occupies the second ledger line above the bass clef staff.

The next song incorporates the high E note on both hands along with some glissando techniques.

Ben Crumples

Grace Notes

The grace note is a wonderful tool you can use to add life to a melody. Used by virtually every other musical instrument, it is equally effective on the piano keyboard. A *grace note* serves as a sort of "lead-in" to a melody note, like a singer starting a half or whole step below target pitch to add some dynamic to the vocal. The grace note is played very quickly and has no rhythmic value. It is notated as a cue-size eighth note with a slash through it. A slur bridges the grace note to its melody note.

Grace Notes

Talkback

St. Louis Blues

Tremolo

The technique of alternating between two interval notes as quickly as possible is called **tremolo.** You can apply tremolo to any musical interval, but the octave tremolo is perhaps the most popular in rock music. Tremolo is notated like this:

The two notes to which the tremolo is applied are notated with the same rhythmic value, but you only count one of them. That is, for a whole-note tremolo, both notes will be notated as whole notes, but the measure only counts as four beats, not eight.

Track 55

Track 56

Track 57

Tremolodeous

Rumba Tumbo

Key of B♭

The key of B♭ contains two flatted notes: B♭ and E♭. As such, the B♭ scale is the first scale you have encountered that starts on a black key. This requires a slight adjustment in the fingering technique for both the right and left hands in both the ascending and descending patterns. For the right hand, start with finger 2 on B♭ and then immediately cross under with finger 1 to play the C note. This is also your first two-octave scale, so pay close attention to the fingerings.

Track 59

B♭ Major Scale

With the left hand, begin with finger 3 and play the first three notes in position. Then, cross over with finger 4 to complete the scale. Notice that the high A note is played with finger 1 and the B♭ immediately following is played with a cross over move by finger 3!

Track 60

B♭ Major Scale

New Chords

The primary chords in the key of B♭ are B♭, E♭, F7, and Gm. The keyboard diagrams below depict the fingerings for each of these chords in the left and right hands.

Right Hand

B♭   E♭   F7   Gm

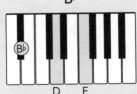
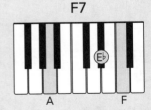
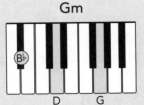

Left Hand

B♭   E♭   F7   Gm

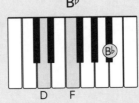
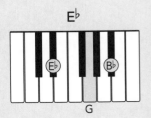
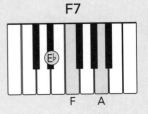
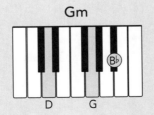

Right Hand

Track 61

Left Hand

Track 62

Alouettah

Track 63

Star Spangled Banner

New Dynamics: *pp, mp, ff*

It's time to expand your dynamic playing by introducing three new sounds: pianissimo, mezzo piano, and fortissimo. The *pianissimo* (*pp*) dynamic marking indicates that you should play the section or song very softly. The *mezzo piano* (*mp*) dynamic marking indicates that you should play moderately loud. The *fortissimo* (*ff*) dynamic marking indicates a very loud section or song. The examples below will demonstrate the difference between the six dynamics you've now learned.

Track 65

Right Hand Dynamics

Track 66

Left Hand Dynamics

Track 67

Miss Dyna

▶ Be sure to adjust your dynamics abrubtly between measures 13 and 17. Practice these measures separately to ensure steady timing.

The Grand Finale

The Labrador from Ecuador

Track 68

Danny Boy

Closing

We hope *Play Piano Today: Level 2* has inspired you to continue in your piano studies. For additional practice material, check out the *Play Piano Today Songbook*, which corresponds to the contents presented in both *Play Piano Today!* volumes.

Play Today!

A Complete Guide to the Basics

THE ULTIMATE SELF-TEACHING SERIES!

How many times have you said: "I wish I would've learned to play guitar… piano… saxophone…" Well, it's time to do something about it. The revolutionary Play Today! Series from Hal Leonard will get you doing what you've always wanted to do: make music. Best of all, with these book/CD packs you can listen and learn at your own pace, in the comfort of your own home!

This method can be used by students who want to teach themselves or by teachers for private or group instruction. It is a complete guide to the basics, designed to offer quality instruction in the book and on the CD, terrific songs, and a professional-quality CD with tons of full-demo tracks and audio instruction. Each book includes over 70 great songs and examples!

PLAY GUITAR TODAY
by Doug Downing
   INCLUDES TAB

_____ 00696100 Level 1 ....$9.95
_____ 00696101 Level 2 ....$9.95

PLAY GUITAR TODAY SONGBOOK
   INCLUDES TAB

Companion songbook to the Play Guitar Today! instructional method with 10 great songs, including: American Pie • Born to Be Wild • Brown Eyed Girl • Every Breath You Take • I Shot the Sheriff • Let It Be • Oh, Pretty Woman • Time Is on My Side • Wild Thing • You Really Got Me.
_____ 00696102 Book/CD Pack $12.95

PLAY GUITAR TODAY – COMPLETE KIT
A great boxed set that includes both Play Guitar Today instruction books, the Play Guitar Today Songbook, and the Grandstand bookstand.
_____ 00695662 ....$29.95

PLAY BASS TODAY
by Chris Kringel
   INCLUDES TAB

_____ 00842020 Level 1 ....$9.95
_____ 00842036 Level 2 ....$9.95

PLAY DRUMS TODAY
by Scott Schroedl
_____ 00842021 Level 1 ....$9.95
_____ 00842038 Level 2 ....$9.95

PLAY PIANO TODAY
by Warren Wiegratz
_____ 00842019 Level 1 ....$9.95
_____ 00842040 Level 2 ....$9.95

PLAY ALTO SAX TODAY
_____ 00842049 Level 1 ....$9.95
_____ 00842050 Level 2 ....$9.95

PLAY FLUTE TODAY
_____ 00842043 Level 1 ....$9.95
_____ 00842044 Level 2 ....$9.95

PLAY CLARINET TODAY
_____ 00842046 Level 1 ....$9.95
_____ 00842047 Level 2 ....$9.95

PLAY TRUMPET TODAY
_____ 00842052 Level 1 ....$9.95
_____ 00842053 Level 2 ....$9.95

FOR MORE INFORMATION, SEE YOUR LOCAL MUSIC DEALER,
OR WRITE TO:

HAL•LEONARD® CORPORATION
7777 W. BLUEMOUND RD. P.O. BOX 13819 MILWAUKEE, WI 53213